FOLLOWING JESUS

trey gilmore

—

ISBN: 9798443706207

To my dad,

who never got to experience Contrast Church.

&

to those faithfully following Jesus in Grandview,

Columbus, and the ends of the Earth.

introduction vi

part one

jesus 10

part two

relationship 20

formation 34

mission 48

community 62

tetelestai 78

appendixes

VIM 80

rule of life 83

recommended reading 90

introduction

And what do you benefit if you gain the whole world but lose your own soul? Is anything worth more than your soul?

- Matthew 16:26 NLT

The Gospel of John, known to be full of both incredible symbolism and theological density, has Jesus' first question being:

> "What do you *want*?"
> - John 1:38a[1]

and his final question being:

> "Do you *love* me?"
> - John 20:17

It is no coincidence that John spends his entire gospel account of Jesus helping explain just how following Jesus flows into our answer to both of these questions.

This is where we must start.

When we are honest with ourselves about these questions, we are able to truly dive into the depths of our souls and find a longing that cannot be satisfied by anything the world has to offer.

> They said to him, "Rabbi [Teacher], where are you staying?" Jesus answered, "Come and you will see."
> - John 1:38b-39a

Andrew (one of the first disciples) and a friend had heard things about this "Jesus guy," which propelled them into a curiosity about who Jesus was. Jesus asked what their hearts desired, and extended an invitation to "come and see." In the same way, we are to "come and see," who Jesus is, what he desires of us, and what we can receive from Him.

Following Jesus is a journey of *reorienting our heart* to Him and His way for life in His kingdom. It is both for now and forever.

But, before we get into this, we need to acknowledge that some of the most difficult barriers to following Jesus are because of his people (those "Christians"). There are no shortages of preconceived notions, experiences, and even trauma that we have all experienced from "Christians" or the Church (myself included). Often, when we try to look at Jesus and who he is, we don't truly see him because we have built up an idea of him based on all of this.

Fortunately for us, when we talk about following Jesus, we don't start with the Church, we start with Him. From there, we join his Mission, and then we get to see our integration and identity in the church.

So, lets jump in and start with the simple, but incredibly powerful question:

Who is Jesus?

—

jesus

In order to follow Jesus, it is really important to first know the basics of Jesus. The best way to get to know Jesus, who he was, and what he did, is to read what was said of him in the Bible. A.W. Tozer once said:

> "What comes into our minds when we think about God is the most important thing about us."[2]

We must see who God is on *his terms*, otherwise our idea of *truth* will primarily be a combination of our own opinion and whatever our feelings dictate. We all know how helpful and beautiful feelings can be, but we also are aware of their tendency to overlook things or act irrationally.

Think about it like this: Imagine that you take a drive, and you are letting off some steam. You are on the highway with a speed limit of 65, but you are cruising at a slick 95 mph. An officer pulls you over, and you start to argue with him. You state that you swear you were doing 65 mph. He is adamant that you were speeding. In this situation, who is right? How can you tell? Anyone with common sense would say, "well if the officer had a speed radar gun, you trust that." Especially if you are going 30 mph over the speed limit.

In the same way, a lot of us have heard things about Jesus, but at the end of the day, we need a radar or a baseline that is able to get to the truth of what we actually need to hear. Otherwise, we are left to our own devices (opinions). I don't know if any of us want to drive on a highway where anyone can go as fast as they want with no speed limit or consequences. In the same way, when everyone gets to create their *own* version of God we have a lot of problems.

—

The Gospels and a Recap
The simplest way to learn about Jesus is to jump into the

gospels accounts of Him in the Bible. There are four of these (Matthew, Mark, Luke, and John) and they're each unique in their vocation, personality, preference, etc.

All four of them give us a detailed account of a man named Jesus. To be honest, this story is quite wild; some would even say unbelievable. So for the sake of being on the same page, let's recap:

We believe that a man named Jesus came to earth, born in the little town of Bethlehem, lived a life like you and me, and was just an ordinary carpenter for most of his life. However, he is both fully-God and fully-man, and was sinless while on earth. Around his early-30s, He stepped into what is known as his "public ministry." He started to perform profound miracles and healings to people all throughout the land. His main priority was to glorify God by proclaiming his coming kingdom, and for us to repent and believe this message. This message was ultimately displayed through his crucifixion, death, burial, and resurrection. It was the final sacrifice that displayed God's power and defeat over sin and death. This message, which we refer to as the Gospel, or the "good news" is available to each one of us.

Even more, we believe that we are given this good news and the gift of eternal life for free. That's right, free. God extends this to us, and not only do we get a restored relationship with God, we also get an eternity with him. We are also his image-bearers here on Earth, being a part of his plan, restoring all things to Him right here, right now. We do this in part by becoming more like him, and teaching others the same. This is the project that anyone who believes in and follows him, is working on while on earth.

If that isn't wild enough, he also *said* and *did* some crazy things. His most popular saying was "repent (turn away), for the kingdom of God is near." Basically, the life you are living is wrong, and causing destruction for you and those around you. Turn away from it, because my own way of life is coming, and it will give you true life. Talk about harsh. That would be like going up to a smoker and yelling: "STOP SMOKING. It's bad for you!" This strategy typically doesn't go over well.

He also told people that his kingdom was full of the very people you would least expect, and that in this kingdom, the rules and ethics were intense. They were harder than anything we have ever had to follow. In His kingdom, he basically flips everything we have known in our power/culture structures upside down. The poor are those who receive this kingdom, the rich are prideful and will be judged harshly. The very people we think about as successful by the world's standards are actually the farthest away from Jesus' kingdom and its values. In fact, he talked about money and wealth a lot. Like half of the time. Spoiler alert… most time he was warning of the dangers of wealth and money.

He also didn't just say these bold things, he lived a life of radical service for others through his life and actions. He performed dozens of supernatural miracles, healed people of physical ailments, cast out demons, raised people from the dead, and more. He became so popular that people would flock into small houses just to hear his words. What does he do? He hides, he retreats, he spends a ton of time in prayer. He goes and hangs out with the social outcasts, those who have nothing to offer him. He goes and spends time with the religious elite too. He is friends with the lowly and the rich. He is loved by the people so much that they try to make him king, but those in power get fearful and try to trick him. They eventually get one of his disciples to betray him, leading him into a painful, lonely, and embarrassing crucifixion. The entire time, Jesus is still faithful to the Father and his mission. So much so, that he is asking for God to forgive his enemies up until his final breath. Then he dies, and it's like the earth shook. Those around him realized this guy wasn't just some 30-year-old Jewish man, but something much greater.

A few days later, in a tomb guarded by thousands of

pounds of stone and dozens of Roman guards, he resurrects, and reveals himself to more than 500 people. Weeks later, he ascends to heaven where he sits beside God the Father until we await his return. In the meantime, he has given us the Holy Spirit to be our aid and advocate.

Whew... I don't know about you, but I can read this and it's easy to think: This is crazy. And you're not wrong; it is. However, would you expect the God of the universe to do things just like you'd expect them? This story, read at face-value, is wild. It's compelling and beautiful, but seems far-fetched, distant, and too-good-to-be-true. The best part about this story though, is the more you immerse yourself in it, the more beautiful, powerful, and fantastic it becomes. The more you fall in love with Jesus, the more you want nothing more than to be in his presence and become like him.

After we read this story, we typically have the train of thought—what does this have to do with me? How am I saved again? How do I get what Jesus' died for and gave us? Don't worry, you aren't alone. The next section will help you to better understand exactly what the good news of the Gospel is.

—

The Gospel (Good News)

> "What must I *do* to be saved?"
> - Acts 16:30

> Now someone came up to him and said, "Teacher, what good thing must I *do* to gain eternal life?"
> - Matthew 19:16

"What must I *do* to be saved?" is one of the most common questions still asked and pondered by many today, including those who would normally call themselves Christians.

First, it might be wise to figure out what Jesus is actually saving us from. If he is saving me from companies trying to reach me about my car's extended warranty then I'm pretty interested! But if it's not something we think we need saving from, chances are we won't really care all that much.

Salvation, simply put, means *deliverance* or *rescuing from peril*. This peril is sin that leads to death. Sin leads us to the absence of God, or us choosing a trajectory without God. He is saving us because though we were created good, we got the keys to run the place and screwed up real bad. Even worse, it is much deeper than we think. Sin isn't just merely an *action*, but a deeply-rooted *heart problem* that has and is damaging our world as we know it. Our hearts are the deepest level our being, some would even describe it as your soul. It is where your deepest inclinations, desires, and longings come from. It is this place where we choose ourselves over God, or treasure anything above God. It is thinking that we know better, or would be a better god than God himself. It is personal, but also on a larger, societal scale too. However, there are some passages that give us hope:

> God therefore, gave his one and only Son, that whoever *believes in him*, should not perish but have eternal life.
> - John 3:16

> God, being rich in mercy because of his great love with which he loved us, even though we were dead in offenses, *made us alive* together with Christ—by grace you are saved!
> - Ephesians 2:4-5

If we *believe* in Jesus, and this message, we receive an eternal trajectory, life, and relationship with Jesus. For many this may seem too simplistic. You can almost hear a little voice saying: "Yeah, but what's the catch!?" It is important that we actually define what it means to believe. Believing in Jesus isn't just believing that he simply *existed*, it is a "belief" that *transcends your intellect into your heart and body*. This means that your desires, passions, and actions start to embrace this belief as a life change. This is where the rubber hits the road. It's all peaches n' cream to say one thing, but to *believe* it so much that it changes, guides, and convicts your entire being is a whole other level of belief. This is why Jesus says:

> "If anyone wants to become my follower, he must deny himself, take up his cross, and follow me."
> - Matthew 16:24

Our faith and belief in Jesus extends into our entire body and soul. We can believe in Jesus and his resurrection from a soul and cerebral level, but we should express it in our actions by "taking up our cross" or living as a true follower of Jesus.

—

Here, and Not Yet

One of the least mentioned components of Jesus is his *kingdom*. It is hard to separate the King from his kingdom. This kingdom Jesus speaks about is giving us the true meaning for our lives on earth. Jesus speaks of a kingdom, which is ruled by him. This kingdom isn't merely physical borders on earth. It has domain in the spiritual realm and extends to the depths of our hearts. The kingdom is where God's domain is being established. Simply put, Jesus' kingdom is his way made a reality through his followers.

Jesus is indeed King, and this kingdom has him, Jesus, as the ruler. His kingdom is a renewing work for the hearts of sinners. However, this kingdom reminds us not just that we are saved *from* sin, but we are saved *for* life, freedom, holiness, and faithfulness. This kingdom reality gives us purpose after initial salvation. We do not simply just wait for Jesus' return, but instead are participating in his active redemption on earth, here and now. Think about this for a second. Imagine that you had a young, best friend and they promised you (no matter what), that you would get to celebrate their 80th birthday with them. Since you're their best friend you are really excited. Now, would you tuck the save-the-date in your pocket and go live your life? Or would you continue to build an even deeper, greater, and more life-giving friendship with that person? You may get to go to the 80th birthday either way. But which choice would make it much more fun and special? Which choice would make the journey better? Jesus isn't into the save-the-dates on your fridge for your life.

John Calvin once said that it is the *task* of the church to make the invisible kingdom visible. We do that by living in such a way that we bear witness to the reality of the kingship of Jesus in our jobs, our families, our schools, and even our checkbooks, because God (Jesus) is King over every one of these spheres of life. The only way the kingdom of God is going to manifest in this world before Jesus returns is if we let Jesus use us in the way we live as citizens of heaven and subjects of the King while on earth.

This is the purpose and call on our lives, and Jesus' priority in his ministry and commissioning to the disciples.

This is Jesus, his priorities, and how we fit into his plan. You may not have realized all of this when you signed up to follow Jesus. It is both the hardest and easiest thing, but it is the best thing you'll ever sign up for.

I want us to spend the next four chapters navigating through four components to following Jesus. These aren't perfectly separate as they intertwine a lot. But these four main areas are what we can best see and understand of following Jesus in John 15.

part two

john fifteen

I am the true vine and my Father is the gardener. He takes away every branch that does not bear fruit in me. He prunes every branch that bears fruit so that it will bear more fruit. You are clean already because of the word that I have spoken to you. Remain in me, and I will remain in you. Just as the branch cannot bear fruit by itself, unless it remains in the vine, so neither can you unless you remain in me. I am the vine; you are the branches. The one who remains in me—and I in him—bears much fruit, because apart from me you can accomplish nothing. If anyone does not remain in me, he is thrown out like a branch, and dries up; and such branches are gathered up and thrown into the fire, and are burned up. If you remain in me and my words remain in you, ask whatever you want, and it will be done for you. My Father is honored by this, that you bear much fruit and show that you are my disciples. Just as the Father has loved me, I have also loved you; remain in my love. If you obey my commandments, you will remain in my love, just as I have obeyed my Father's commandments and remain in his love. I have told you these things so that my joy may be in you, and your joy may be complete. My commandment is this—to love one another just as I have loved you. No one has greater love than this—that one lays down his life for his friends. You are my friends if you do what I command you. I no longer call you slaves, because the slave does not understand what his master is doing. But I have called you friends, because I have revealed to you everything I heard from my Father. You did not choose me, but I chose you and appointed you to go and bear fruit, fruit that remains, so that whatever you ask the Father in my name he will give you. This I command you—to love one another.

—

relationship

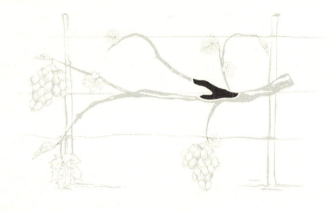

Remain in me, and I will remain in you. Just as the branch cannot bear fruit by itself, unless it remains in the vine, so neither can you unless you remain in me. I am the vine; you are the branches. The one who remains in me—and I in him—bears much fruit because apart from me you can accomplish nothing. If anyone does not remain in me, he is thrown out like a branch and dries up; and such branches are gathered up and thrown into the fire and are burned up.

- John 15:4-6

When someone comes to follow Jesus in the Western world, it can be very easy to have a cerebral belief in God (and Jesus), but have very little, if any, relationship with Him. This is because that's how our world, society, and culture around us works. We esteem the intelligent and hard-working and have very little time for the internal heart of things, especially because they can be hard to quantify. It is much more apparent when someone works 80 hours in a week and has money, possessions, and fame to show for it. On the flip side, people see very little from you spending an hour on your knees in prayer in your room each day. But, we know that following Jesus is far more than just knowing and doing. It is truly about being with Him. God is a personal being, and reveals his priority for relationship in the Trinity. We are human *beings*, not human *doings*.

If someone is married, being a great spouse wouldn't entail just knowing things about their spouse and doing things for them. What would be far greater is your relational strength, and the depth/intimacy of your relationship. Now this may be hard to "count" but fairly easy to "feel." In the same way, we are only able to follow Jesus in a deeper way if we are spending time being with Him.

For some of you this may even seem juvenile or basic. Well of course, following Jesus means that we are to be with Jesus, that we are to be in relationship with him. But as one of my favorite pastor and author, the late Dallas Willard once said:

> "Few people arise in the morning as hungry for God as they are for cornflakes or toast and eggs."[3]

I would add a nice coffee (Kenyan pour over to be precise). But regardless, it seems like an obvious point: be in relationship with Jesus.

But if I was to ask you, "how is that relationship going," what would you say? Would you respond in such a way that showed you are placing Jesus at the priority of each day? Or is he squeezing into your schedule?

Would you respond in such a way that it is clear Jesus is doing continual work on your heart and in your life? Or are you comfortable with the way everything is, as if you've arrived at the American "Christian" status and you're on autopilot?

Would you respond in such a way that you only can equivocate your relationship with Jesus based on the works and things you are doing at your church, the money you give away, or hours you serve?

Again, if you were to tell me about a relationship in your life that was growing and becoming closer and more intimate, say a significant other, parent or a best friend. Would your answer simply be all the things that you do for them? Surely not! The deepening of your relationship would include the spending of time, but it wouldn't *just be* the spending of time (you can spend a whole day with someone and still not be present with and for them). It would be better measured by the excitement and depth of the relationship and would probably be explained far better by how well they know you and you know them. How well they *know you*. Your quirks, desires, dreams, and fears. How secure can you feel with them? How trustworthy have they proven to be? What is your communication and intimacy like?

If I was to ask you, what does it mean to *be with Jesus,* what would you say?

Our relationship with Jesus is the most powerful thing in our lives.. It is not a transactional acquaintance, but a *union* with him as we become like Him through the Holy Spirit's power.

Richard Foster, a spiritual discipline expert, says that:

> "The desperate need today is not for a greater number of intelligent people, or gifted people, but for deep people."[4]

Some of you may not even know that Jesus has the desire to be in a personal *relationship* and *union* with each of us. But I also think that many of us may not even realize that a relationship could mean a two-way, conversational, intimate, and consistent relationship with Jesus. Something as real as a one-on-one coffee meetup with the best of friends or family member.

Here is the skinny of why this is important and must be addressed first:

> We are only able to love others well, to be a part of the mission of God, and more, from an outpouring of our relationship with Jesus.

Yes, we can do a bunch of things for God, but still not be with God. Works, achievements and accomplishments aren't the *foundation*, they are the *fruit* of union with Jesus.

In Luke 10, Jesus comes to stay with sisters, Martha and Mary. While Martha was all-busy trying to work for Jesus, Mary was at the feet of Jesus enthralled by Him and his words. Mary was soaking up his teachings and in that culture sitting at the feet of a "rabbi" was communicating a passionate student wanting to learn. What was Jesus' response to the contrasting priorities?

> "Martha, Martha, you are worried and troubled about many things, but one thing is needed. Mary has chosen the best part; it will not be taken away from her."
> - Luke 10:41-42.

Jesus also says in a different passage:

> "Not everyone who says to me, 'Lord, Lord,' will enter into the kingdom of heaven—only the one who does the will of my Father in heaven. On that day, many will say to me, 'Lord, Lord, didn't we prophesy in your name, and cast out demons in your name, and do many powerful deeds in your name?' Then I will

declare to them, '*I never knew you*. Go away from me, you lawbreakers!"
   - Matthew 7:21-23

Jesus says "I never knew you." Our relationship with Jesus is more than merely doing, it is being with Him, in what Pete Scazzero describes as, "a loving union." He says:

> *Love* captures the way we remain in Jesus. *Union* speaks to the depth of the connection with Him.[5]

—

Jesus' Relationship with the Father is Our Plumb Line
I grew up playing tennis on a clay court. For you it may be rare or even unheard of, but I loved getting to slide around as I played each summer. Unfortunately, being on clay meant having plastic lines that must be nailed down each spring for a new year of tennis. You would haul tons (I mean literally tons) of new clay in, spread it and lay the lines. If you've ever wondered how the lines are so straight, you would take precise measurements, then you would get out this contraption called a "plumb bob." It was essentially a string that was loaded with chalk. You would take the string from one end to the other, lay it down, and SNAP. It would place a clean straight line for reference once the nailing of the lines started. You do this because once you get on your knees, put your head down and start nailing it can be easy to lose track of where you are going and veer off-course if you don't have a reference. This chalkline was the central focus or the standard for knowing how we were doing. A chalk-line, or a similarly used "plumb line" helps keep us centered and on course. We should use Jesus' relationship with His Father as a plumb line for our relationship with Him.

If you read the "red letters" in your Bible, you will quickly become attuned to what the incredible dependence of Jesus on his Father looked like. We typically use dependency in a clinical, negative way. You are dependent on someone, your spouse, or you are codependent with your mom, or kids. These are signs of being unhealthy because they assume that the point of being human is to be *independent*, and ideally not dependent on anything. That is a strength in our culture. The idea then moves deeper from independence, to *interdependence* (being independent together). However, when we look at Jesus and his Father, he may be the most *dependent* person who has ever existed. In fact, Paul Miller, in his book *A Praying Life* explains this powerfully:

> Imagine asking Jesus how he's doing. He'd say, "My Father and I are doing great. He has given me everything I need today." You respond, "I'm glad your Father is doing well, but let's just focus on you for a minute. Jesus, how are you doing?" Jesus would look at you strangely, as if you were speaking a foreign language. The question doesn't make sense. He simply can't answer the question "How are you doing?" without including his heavenly Father...[6]

Whenever Jesus starts talking about his relationship with his heavenly Father, Jesus becomes childlike, very *dependent*. "The Son can do nothing of his own accord" (John 5:19). "I can do nothing on my own" (John 5:30). "I do nothing on my own authority, but speak just as the Father taught me" (John 8:28). "The Father who sent me has himself given me . . . what to say and what to speak" (John 12:49).

Jesus' relationship with his Father is our plumb line for our relationship with Him. We get the understanding of an intimate union with Him from his union with the Trinity—Father, Son and Holy Spirit.

—

Relationship is Our Foundation and Nutrition
Jesus is our example of this, he didn't just come to Earth

and work like a madman every day healing as many people as he could. If I told you that you have three years to save the world in your thirties what would you spend time doing now? I would probably study to become a scientist to find a cure for cancer, or maybe start practicing my public speaking skills (after all, you'll have to speak to billions of people).

What does Jesus do?

He spends loads of time in relationship with his Father. Out of his *relationship* came his *ministry* and *mission*. Not the other way around.

Remember, apart from Jesus you cannot do anything. Sure you can try, but anytime I've gotten "ahead" of Jesus while we are walking, it doesn't work out for me. Don't believe me? Head into the forest with your dog, let them off the leash a hundred yards ahead of you and see if they don't get themselves in some trouble.

If Jesus' priority was time spent in relationship, ours should be no different. We may ask ourselves, why was that his priority? As said earlier, if you are going to save the world, wouldn't you get going on saving? One of the wildest things we see in Jesus' lifestyle and rhythms is his *unhurried* and *non-anxious presence*. The God of the universe is not busy or worried. He is so unhurried that he creates an *entire day* (see Genesis 2) for him to rest and bask in his handiwork.

Jesus is unhurried and slow because he is modeling how we prioritize relationships, but he is also receiving the instruction, nutrients and plan from God in this as well. He receives health, clarity, discernment and wisdom in his time with the Father. The best part? We become beneficiaries of those things too. John 15:9 says "Just as the Father has loved me, I have also loved you; remain in my love. This illustration of a vine in John 15 gives us a provocative image of oneness. How can you tell where the vine begins and ends? It's almost impossible. It is all one, and its nutrients and care are given to the entire tree. The Father is the gardener, Jesus is the vine, and from Jesus we are the branches. Jesus is in relationship with the Father, and out of that we are given relationship to Jesus. If we remain in Jesus then we have life. This is a foundational truth of the gospel and following Jesus.

Ephesians 2:18 says that Jesus: "came and preached peace to you who were far off and peace to those who were near, so that *through him* we both have access in one Spirit to the Father.

See, this wasn't a reality before. The Jewish way prior had to have a bunch of sacrificial procedures to even enter close to God's presence, and it was not accessible for everyone. But with Jesus' death, and his taking of our sins, we are one with Jesus, and therefore have full access to the Father.

The good news is not just that he *saved us from sin and death*, but that he is here, living with us now, and that God chooses to be in an intimate relationship with each of us to *continue His work while we are here on Earth*. He is not distant, he is not far off only coming to yell and punish. He is nearer than we could ever imagine.

But, we must *be with Jesus* before we expect to become like Him and live out his mission. It is in our relationship that we start to yearn for following him (or apprenticing him) and that is what changes our lives.

—

Jesus and the Most Important Commandment

There was immense tension as Jesus started to reveal who he was and his truth, the good news. It started to rub against the tradition, the security and the culture that had been created by the Jews. Before Jesus, God had given laws to the Israelites (the Jews) so that they might be able to better understand God's holiness and how to follow him and condemn sin (or things in resistance to God and his plan). However, these Jews had their security so strongly in God's laws and not God himself. They valued the knowledge of law over the heart of God. Though the law was a good thing, it became their priority to their detriment. So Jesus starts to shatter their norm and their traditions. He tells them that the priority of the law was to reveal our hearts desires, not just to create rules, laws, and only pursue head knowledge. We must realize that:

> "Jesus is a teacher who doesn't just inform our *intellect* but forms our very *loves*. He isn't content to simply deposit new ideas into your mind; he is after nothing less than your wants, your loves, your longings."
> - James KA Smith

Our minds are good and helpful (more on that in the next chapter), but they are not the end all. What Jesus wants most is our heart. Our heart is best understood, revealed, and grown in relationships. The smart, religious leaders were more consumed with the intellect and rigidity of the law that they missed the heart of the gospel and why Jesus came. They were consistently trying to attack Jesus' ushering in of this new reality. This reality is incredibly clear in this story:

> Now when the Pharisees heard that he had silenced the Sadducees, they assembled together. And one of them, an expert in religious law, asked him a question to test him: "Teacher, which commandment in the law is the greatest?" Jesus said to him, " 'Love the Lord your God with all your heart, with all your soul, and with all your mind.' This is the first and greatest commandment. The second is like it: 'Love your neighbor as yourself.' All the law and the prophets depend on these two commandments."
> - Matthew 22:34-40

This is a unique situation in that the question being posed was a common question of thought for the religious elite. There were 613 laws that they followed, and there was a constant tension towards which were more important than others. This question posed to Jesus was really posed because it didn't have a right answer, meaning that whichever one he picked might have some agreeing, but others feeling alienated, or vice versa. There was no pleasing everyone.

So Jesus answers the question, but he gives two answers as one.

His first answer is obvious: He recites Deuteronomy 6:8-9, also known as the *Shema*. The *Shema* was recited two times a day by most serious Jews. This commandment when placed alone makes it obvious that our priority is to Love God first. However, in stating his second answer, he is saying that loving our neighbor as ourselves means that it must go hand and hand with the first command. Yes, love for God is first, but the second commandment is only understood in light of the foundation of the first.

This too echoes that concept that we can only truly pursue mission and ministry from the health of our relationship with God first and foremost. Our relationship with Jesus is the well from which everything else flows. Paul Miller says:

> When Jesus tells us that "apart from me you can do nothing" (John 15:5), he is inviting us into his life of a living *dependence* on his heavenly Father. When Jesus tells us to believe, he isn't asking us to work up some spiritual energy. He is telling us to realize that, like him, we don't have the resources to do life. When you know that you (like Jesus) can't do life on your own, then *prayer [relationship] makes complete sense.*[7]

—

How to Strengthen Our Relationship with Jesus
The Bible says that the Holy Spirit will be your advocate in relation to Jesus, and that through the Holy Spirit you will grow deeper into a relationship with Jesus (John 14). But that doesn't just mean we sit aside passively. We are to

participate in this relationship, like any other relationship.

If someone decides that they'd like to be a dancer, do they sit and wait to just become a dancer? If someone wants to be healthy, do they just keep eating junk and staying sedentary? No.

Our spiritual health, and relationship is no different. The Holy Spirit will do work in your life, and place opportunities and convictions on your heart, but you also must be in tune with and walk with the Holy Spirit.

There are many pathways to encountering and growing in relationship. But for the sake of this book's simplicity, we are going to hone in on the most foundational one.

Prayer.

Prayer is the gateway to relationship and intimacy with Jesus. The most effective question someone can ask you about your spiritual journey is: "how is your prayer life?" Richard Foster says that prayer is:

> "the *central avenue* God uses to transform us...If we are unwilling to change, we will abandon prayer as a noticeable characteristic of our lives. The closer we come to the heartbeat of God the more we see our need and the more we desire to be conformed to Christ."[8]

Robert Bakke says:

> "Through prayer we pour our lives, our thoughts, our longings into God and receive the life, power, character, mind, and authority of God in return."[9]

Prayer strengthens our relationship with Jesus, and helps us eliminate the pursuit of that which is temporary, futile, and meaningless. Henri Nouwen says:

> "We want to move closer to God, the source and goal

of our existence, but at the same time we realize that the closer we come to God the stronger will be his demand to *let go* of the many "safe" structures we have built around ourselves. Prayer is such a radical act because it requires us to *criticize our whole way of being in the world*, to lay down our old selves and accept our new self, which is Christ. . . . Prayer therefore is the act of *dying* to all that we consider to be our own and of being born to a new existence which is not of this world."[10]

Ultimately, prayer connects us with Jesus because it places our security, our desires and wants into his hands and allows us to trust that he will do a better job with them than us. This is why prayer is so countercultural. No one wants to spend time giving their security away, they want to spend time bolstering it by doing things others can see and be impressed by. The very act of setting aside time to pray is already anointing time for God to love you. Prayer is the most powerful thing we can do.

There once was a community which was led by Count Zinzendorf, who was well known for the Moravian revival. This community, known as *Herrnhut*, decided to be in constant prayer for their community and the global church 24/7. This was commissioned by 24 men and women who, with the help of their community continued this for *a hundred straight years*.

The results, many authors say, are unexplainable. It was a heaven on Earth community, they were the catalyst for several massive world-size gospel movements and missionaries. Relationship is what Jesus is all about and prayer is the gateway to relationship.

From that, we start to become more like him.

—

Reflection Question
Am I actively believing that the most important thing is

relationship with Christ in the way I spend my time, energy, resources, and love?

Recommended Reading
- *The Praying Life* by Paul E. Miller
- *The Power of Extraordinary Prayer* by Robert Bakke
- *Emotionally Healthy Spirituality* by Pete Scazzero
- *Sacred Pathways* by Gary Thomas
- *In the Name of Jesus* by Henri Nouwen

formation

He takes away every branch that does not bear fruit in me. He prunes every branch that bears fruit so that it will bear more fruit…If you remain in me and my words remain in you, ask whatever you want, and it will be done for you… If you obey my commandments, you will remain in my love, just as I have obeyed my Father's commandments and remain in his love

- John 15:2, 7, 10

"The most profound yearning of the human spirit, which we try to fill with all sorts of inadequate substitutes, is the yearning for our completeness in the image of Christ."[11]

- M. Robert Mulholland

Charles Blondin was a famous daredevil, but especially in the realm of tightrope walking. He would walk across anywhere on a tightrope. He is most famously known for walking across Niagara falls, at 1100 ft (about three football fields). He not only did this daring feat, but he came back across from the Canadian side with a giant camera, and took a photo in the middle. After this day, he promised another performance on the Fourth of July, which he then did without a pole, and at one point flipped upside-down and walked backwards for part of it. He came back again with a sack over his entire body. He did it again a few weeks later with a wheelbarrow, and one time he even cooked and ate an omelet on the rope.

All of these seem more daring than the first, and at some point, we have to conclude that this isn't even hard for him anymore. However, there is one moment, one question that elevates the daring feat of Charles Blondin more than all the rest.

After having successfully crossed all these times, he looks at the crowd and he asks:

"Now, who wants to get on my back while I cross again?"

There was utter silence among all the fans. How can a group of people be so passionate about someone, and believe in what he did, and then be silent when he invites them into such a communal thing with him? We can believe in something, but when the rubber hits the road, will we participate in becoming like Jesus by acting out our trust just like that crowd with Blondin? Jesus is extending his hand, and he is asking:

"Will you get on my back?"

Jesus' Heart
One of the most profound and intimate glimpses we have into Jesus' heart is in Matthew 11:

> Come to me, all you who are weary and burdened, and I will give you rest. Take my yoke on you and learn from me because I am gentle and humble in heart, and you will find rest for your souls. For my yoke is easy to bear, and my load is not hard to carry.
> - Matthew 11:28-30

"Will you take on my yoke?"

This question is one of the hardest and easiest questions that we are asked. It is the hardest because it requires the utmost sacrifice. It requires a "denying of ourselves to take up our own cross," (Matthew 16:24)— our own version of suffering and persecution like that of Jesus. It is the easiest because it is an easy yoke and a light load that allows us to learn from Jesus' perfect heart which will give us ultimate rest for our souls.

This is one of the only instances where Jesus tells us directly what is in his heart: gentleness and humility. To see and learn from this, we must accept the call of self-denial into the formation, or apprenticeship of Jesus.

—

The Western Dilemma
The radical call to be a student/apprentice/follower of

Jesus is much richer than just believing in Jesus, similar to the fans who loved Charles Blondin. They believed in him and his capabilities, but when he asked them to follow him and trust in him, there was silence.

So before we get into what it looks like to take this yoke upon us, I want to help answer the questions:

Why do we have to do anything?
Why become like him?
Why isn't just believing in Jesus all that matters?

This was Jesus' first priority. Look at John revealing this perfectly, as he explains the gospel message by saying:

> Now this is the gospel message we have heard from him and announce to you: God is light, and in him there is no darkness at all. If we say we have fellowship with him and yet keep on walking in the darkness, we are lying and not *practicing the truth*. But if we walk in the light as he himself is in the light, we have fellowship with one another and the blood of Jesus his Son cleanses us from all sin.
> - 1 John 1:5–7

We are to walk hand and hand with Jesus, because in him we have the light, and we are able to walk in the light. This is what we are to believe, to place our faith in. That Jesus was killed and resurrected for us to be reconciled into a relationship with God. But the key phrase is "practicing the truth." It is one thing to *know* the truth, but it is far greater to *practice* the truth.

Our priority in belief is not just a cerebral affirmation of the existence of Jesus. We must be careful with this. We are not just affirming that Jesus was a real man who lived in the first century. Even an atheist-historian would be foolish to deny Jesus existed as a man in the world. There is really no debate that Jesus was a man on earth.

So, just believing that God is real isn't a full belief in

Him as Lord, Savior, and Teacher.

—

Are We Different Than Demons?
James, Jesus' half-brother, says:

> You believe that God is one; well and good. Even the demons believe that—and tremble with fear.
> - James 2:19

The key to understanding our difference from demons is what it means to believe and have faith in Jesus and his redemptive work.

In fact, the Greek word used in most of the New Testament (NT) for the word "faith" was *pistis*. This was used hundreds of times in the NT, and it wasn't just a cerebral belief, but more so an assumption into action and embodiment.

The simplest way to illustrate this is with a chair. I can go around telling everyone how I believe in this chair. Now that could mean that I believe this chair is real. It could, on an even deeper level, mean that I believe this chair will do what it was made and designed to do; hold me up. However, when the Bible talks about "placing our faith in Jesus," "to trust in Him," "to practice the truth," and "to believe in his words," this is more than just saying he is real, much like affirming the chair's existence. It is also more than just saying you believe in all the chair is capable of doing (even the demons believe in this). It is placing your trust in the chair by sitting on it. You are acting out the verb of faith, *pistis,* as well as displaying your faith and trust in the chair by sitting on it.

So, when we say we believe in Jesus, we trust in him, and we place our faith in him, we are most able to show this, to reveal this, to be loyal to him and his love by leaning into Him in such a way of *action*.

"I believe in Jesus." means:

I believe in his words, his teachings, his life, his power, his salvation through God's grace, and his mission placed upon us, *and* I am able to show this by acting upon it. We aren't just to believe he is real, but to place our faith in what he said, did, and called us to do.

Belief is like betting it all. By the very action of betting, you are *showing* that you have full, utmost confidence in what you are betting. You don't even need to use words, your actions speak for themselves

—

The "Get-Out-of-Hell" Card
Many of us can be guilty of treating Jesus like a "get-out-of-jail free card" in Monopoly. It is easy to just claim the existence of God without believing it in a way that changes your life. You get all the "perks" without any conviction or life-change. There is no transformation happening in your life, nor a passion to live for Jesus. It is actually ironic, because in this way of thinking you are admitting you need saving from your current life, only to then keep living the same life that required the saving in the first place. You want the King's stuff without living in his Kingdom with Him. You want a marriage, but don't want to live in the same house or share the same bank account.

We know that is a dangerous place to land. The apathy of Christians in America is currently the devil's most prominent work. He doesn't need to give you sickness, he can just give you an iPhone. Many think the devil works in obvious ways, like plagues, and sickness, or really bad things like abuse or job loss. While these things are transpired by the enemy, some of they most insidious work is to just distract you from the worship, joy, and presence of God, without us really knowing it. As C.S. Lewis once famously said through his allegorical "head-demon" Screwtape:

> "A *moderated* religion is as good for us [the demons] as no religion at all—and more amusing." (p. 46)

You are either all in or all out. Another "in-between" is just an opportunity for evil to fester and manipulate. Most of the time, it can be as subtle as taking intrinsically good things, and making them your everything. Fundamentally, it is a worship of the *creation* instead of the *creator*.

This is the ability to pursue comfort over growth, enabling sin over true love for people, passiveness over confrontation, hypocrisy over grace, or fear over trust and so on.

We cannot be in a true relationship with Jesus without becoming more like Him. When we decide to follow Jesus, the cost is *everything*. The cost is dying to ourselves, and being fully alive in Christ.

—

Jesus' Vine Gives Us All We Need to Grow

The vine analogy in the previous chapter continues this idea. Every single nutrient that we receive as a branch comes from the vine. Therefore, if we believe in Jesus, we are grafted on to his vine, and then our only option is to grow fruit from his nutrients and supply. James says in a longer passage:

> What good is it, my brothers and sisters, if someone claims to have faith but does not have works? Can this kind of faith save him? If a brother or sister is poorly clothed and lacks daily food, and one of you says to them, "Go in peace, keep warm and eat well," but you do not give them what the body needs, what good is it? So also faith, if it does not have works, is dead being by itself. But someone will say, "You have faith and I have works." Show me your faith without works and I will show you faith by my works. You believe that God is one; well and good. *Even the demons believe*

that—and tremble with fear.

> But would you like evidence, you empty fellow, that faith without works is useless? Was not Abraham our father justified by works when he offered Isaac his son on the altar? You see that his *faith was working together with his works and his faith was perfected by works.*
> - James 2:14-22

This passage is showing us that our faith is shown and displayed by our actions, our "sitting on the chair."

However, we must remind ourselves that the works themselves are not what save us. Look back to Ephesians 2:

> For by grace you are saved through faith, and this is not from yourselves, it is the *gift of God*; it is *not from works*, so that no one can boast.
> - Ephesians 2:8-9

We are not slaves to doing good, or being better, or doing things to impress God. We are not playing a scale of good and bad so that if we do more things good than bad then our belief looks real. We must understand the difference between becoming more like Jesus with a *religious* mindset and a *gospel* mindset.

Religion, or legalism, says that:
    We must obey Him and perform works, and therefore we are accepted and loved by Him.

But the gospel, the belief in Jesus, is:
    We are loved and accepted *first*, therefore we would love to obey and live as he did.

We want to obey and live as he did because our entire trajectory wants nothing more than Jesus, his Kingdom, and his will to be done in, through, and around us.

Our faith and belief must be rooted in *his love*, and not in our effort. Our faith in belief rooted in the love and grace of God is then the fuel and foundation for our displaying of faith/belief in our lives.

—

What Does it Mean to Become like Jesus?

> But whoever obeys his word, truly in this person the love of God has been perfected. By this we know that we are in him. The one who says he resides in God ought himself to *walk just as Jesus walked*.
> - 1 John 2:5-6

Therefore, becoming like Jesus, or spiritual formation (being formed into the image of Christ), is to *walk just as Jesus walked*.

The start of spiritual formation is the death of self. It is to choose death and to take up our cross as Jesus would. Therefore, we can't expect to become more like Jesus if we aren't able to first acknowledge our brokenness, shortcomings, and the need for his grace.

With this continual acknowledgment, and our relationship with Jesus as our foundation, we are called to become more and more like Jesus.

Our Spiritual formation and becoming more like Jesus is really focusing on two areas:

1. Know him (what he said, taught, believed, prioritized, loved).

2. Do what he did and would do if he were you.

Dallas Willard says,

> "discipleship (or spiritual formation) is "the process of *becoming* who Jesus would *be* if He were you."

In doing this, rooted in our relationship with Jesus, we usher in a display of the Kingdom of God for others to see and join. This is why Jesus didn't heal just for numbers, and didn't spend every day grinding out miracles. His priority was bringing a message that he would also model for us as the life we should all seek to live.

He spent three years displaying the beauty, freedom, joy, and love that the Kingdom of God is filled with. Now we are to help fulfill the emulation of this Kingdom by modeling the same way he did it.

Spiritual formation isn't an optional piece to following Jesus, it is the way to understanding and revealing Jesus and his Kingdom here and now, so that you are *practicing for eternity*. Eternity after our physical death is a spiritual eternity in relationship with Jesus in his Kingdom. So we should probably get used to that now.

—

Spiritual formation is the work of the Holy Spirit

Most of us know what to do, but we can't do it. We also know what not to do, but still do those very things. Be comforted, you are not alone. The apostle Paul had the same struggle in Romans 7, as he says he cannot seem to do what he wants, but instead what he hates. What he hates, he does.

Yes, we are made new in Christ, and there is no condemnation for those in Christ. But, we must not forget that we are still at battle with the world, flesh and sin while here.

So growing in our spiritual formation is first and foremost a work of the Holy Spirit dwelling in our hearts, renovating our loves and desires. As mentioned earlier, it is not just passive, but it is our participation and co-laboring with the Holy Spirit that is so crucial. We must yearn for the Spirit to work and grow us in our formation. This yearning though, is rooted in the gospel and relationship with Jesus.

I love Jesus' mini explanation of what the kingdom of heaven is like:

> "The kingdom of heaven is like a treasure, hidden in a field, that a person found and hid. Then because of joy he went and *sold all that he had* and bought that field."
> - Matthew 13:44

Our vision for the gospel and the kingdom should move us to intentions that place everything below the importance of Jesus and his kingdom. We don't just see the treasure and think,
"Well that is cool, I'll leave it there and do nothing about it."
If we are able to see and understand the value of the treasure, we will leverage every area of our lives to make sure we secure that treasure because we know its worth.

> "Those who are not genuinely convinced that the only real bargain in life is surrendering ourselves to Jesus and his cause, abandoning all that we love to him and from him, *cannot* learn the other lessons Jesus has to teach us."[12]
> - Dallas Willard

He uses the analogy:

> "If I tell you that you cannot drive an automobile unless you can see, I'm not saying I will not let you, but good luck driving without being able to see at all."[13]

It is focused entirely on Jesus, and its goal is obedience to Jesus that comes from an inner transformation of our hearts and minds.
Jesus came proclaiming to all to: "Repent! For the Kingdom of God is here!" Therefore, union and

relationship with him by grace (unblemished access to God), are possible through what he did on the cross. But, what made his proclamation so powerful is that it was backed up by his presence, actions, and teachings.

His disciples were formed into who they were by Jesus reaching their *hearts*, changing their *vision* of reality, and their *intentions* for life through tangible, practical *means*.

—

Getting on Jesus' Back

"Who wants to get on my back while I cross again?"

Back to Blondin the Daredevil, as the silence of his fans continued, finally one man decided to be brave enough to follow his call. It was a man by the name of Harry Colcord. Colcord was his *manager*. He had spent hours watching his daredevil, he knew his seriousness, his talents, the time he had spent practicing, he had spent immense time with him, and truly trusted Blondin. When Colcord got on his back, Blondin said this:

> "Look up, Harry... you are no longer Colcord, you are Blondin. Until I clear this place be a part of me, mind, body, and soul. If I sway, sway with me. Do not attempt to do any balancing yourself. If you do we will both go to our death."[14]

Becoming more like Jesus is rooted in a call to following him, taking his yoke, and yielding to the Spirit. It is this beautiful loving union that we see. Don't try doing it yourself, don't root it in our effort, be a part of the vine-- mind, body, and soul, and you'll become more and more like Jesus. And in this, we will learn what it truly means to believe in Jesus, be with him in relationship, and become more and more like him.

Reflection Question
Am I yielding to the Spirit and co-laboring with him to cultivating a heart, head, and body that are more like Jesus each day?

Recommended Reading
- *Renovation of the Heart* by Dallas Willard
- *The Cost of Discipleship* by Dietrich Bonhoeffer
- *Celebration of Discipline* by Richard Foster
- *Gentle & Lowly* by Dane Ortlund
- *The Ruthless Elimination of Hurry* by John Mark Comer
- *Invitation to a Journey: A Road Map for Spiritual Formation* by M. Robert Mulholland Jr.

mission

My commandment is this—to love one another just as I have loved you. No one has greater love than this—that one lays down his life for his friends. You are my friends if you do what I command you. I no longer call you slaves, because the slave does not understand what his master is doing. But I have called you friends, because I have revealed to you everything I heard from my Father. You did not choose me, but I chose you and appointed you to go and bear fruit, fruit that remains, so that whatever you ask the Father in my name he will give you. This I command you—to love one another.

- John 15:12-17

Now that we've rooted ourselves in Jesus and our relationship with him, while leaning into spiritual formation, we are able to pursue the *mission* of Jesus in our lives.

The best place to start when considering Jesus' mission for us is to answer:

What was Jesus' *own* mission on earth?

Or maybe, better-yet: "What is God's mission entirely?" Jesus is certainly at the center, but we must not forget the Old Testament and God's mission there because it directly correlates to the coming and mission of Jesus.
As a reminder, there are four different accounts (Matthew, Mark, Luke and John) of Jesus' life, ministry, death and resurrection that really give us a full picture of his own mission.

John starts off his gospel account immediately stating that: Jesus is the light, that he is the truth and grace, and from him, he takes away the sins of the world.[15] Therefore, we know that Jesus himself became flesh so that he might become like us to die for us. Jesus' primary mission was to *display fulfilled love*, to become human and die for our sins. In this he fulfills the laws that atoned from sin. John blatantly and consistently uses love as the means of mission and says:

> …God is *love*. By this the *love* of God is revealed in us: that God has sent his one and only Son into the world so that we may live through him. And this is *love*: not that we have *loved* God, but that he *loved* us and sent his Son to be the atoning sacrifice for our sins. Dear friends, if God so *loved* us, then we also ought to *love* one another
> - 1 John 4:8-11

However, Dr. Luke's introduction focuses more on the *fulfillment* aspect of love. The beginning of Jesus' ministry, and his mission show us this:

> Now Jesus came to Nazareth, where he had been brought up, and went into the synagogue on the Sabbath day, as was his custom. He stood up to read, and the scroll of the prophet Isaiah was given to him. He unrolled the scroll and found the place where it was written,
> "The Spirit of the Lord is upon me,
> because he has anointed me to proclaim good news to the poor. He has sent me to proclaim release to the captives and the regaining of sight to the blind, to set free those who are oppressed, to proclaim the year of the Lord's favor."
> Then he rolled up the scroll, gave it back to the attendant, and sat down. The eyes of everyone in the synagogue were fixed on him. Then he began to tell them, "Today this scripture has been fulfilled even as you heard it being read." All were speaking well of him, and were amazed at the gracious words coming out of his mouth.
> - Luke 4:16-22

In this passage, Jesus is reading from Isaiah 61:1-2 (& 58:6) This is essentially a mic drop to the listeners because they had known the prophecies of Isaiah which they were awaiting to be fulfilled. They had read this all the time at the synagogue. All the sudden Jesus comes up to read it and says after:

> "Today, this scripture has been fulfilled."

So Jesus is testifying to his own ministry by the reading of Isaiah in front of everyone. He then says, I am here to fulfill this. Isaiah has several prophetic statements that Jesus fulfills, and even the apostle Paul quotes Isaiah in Acts saying:

For this is what the Lord has commanded us: "I have appointed you to be a light for the Gentiles [us], to bring salvation to the ends of the earth."
 - Acts 13:47

Jesus' Mission Fulfills the OT Mission
We cannot separate God's intentions for his kingdom in the Old Testament, because Jesus fulfills it in the New Testament. He doesn't erase everything and start over. He fulfills it and calls people deeper from the *law* of God into the *heart* of God. All of the book of Acts and Paul's letters are centered around the church and their strengths and weaknesses as they spread the gospel.
Jesus' mission of love is to prioritize two displays of this love:

1. *Proclaim* the good news (the Kingdom of heaven is near) and the Lord's favor,

The Gospel is the "good news," and in Jesus' ministry, it is access into the Kingdom of God (heaven) which is God reigning in the lives of those who repent and place faith in Christ. Again, Jesus' primary message was: Repent, for the kingdom of heaven is near. In John 4, the woman at the well proclaims what Jesus did for her to the town she resided in, and people were saved from her proclamation about Jesus.

2. Set free the captives and oppressed through his transforming *presence*.

This is done through his love, his grace, his mercy, his teaching (parables), his lifestyle, and his power (miracles). These two go practically hand and hand together. There are several instances where Jesus *heals* people so that he reveals his ability to *forgive* sins, i.e. to set the captives and oppressed free.

Jesus teaches what we call his upside-down kingdom in a massive teaching section called the Sermon on the Mount (Matt. 5-7) and his first priority in this sermon is to mention the inclusivity of all. It is to flip the cultural standards for who would normally get preference for a kingdom (access by money, status, or power) and instead by trust in Him that leads to sacrifice, self-giving love, humility, and service.

Jesus' mission is establishing the love of God to be tangibly seen and understood through the *presence* in his ministry that reveals the reality of the Kingdom of heaven for those on earth, and His *proclamation* for people to hear and respond.

—

Jesus' Extends His Mission to His Apostles

In Matthew 10, we see Jesus sending out his Twelve Apostles to do His mission:

> Jesus called his twelve disciples and gave them authority over unclean spirits so they could cast them out and heal every kind of disease and sickness...Jesus sent out these twelve, instructing them as follows: "Do not go to Gentile regions and do not enter any Samaritan town. Go instead to the lost sheep of the house of Israel. As you go, preach this message: 'The kingdom of heaven is near!' Heal the sick, raise the dead, cleanse lepers, cast out demons. Freely you received, freely give. Do not take gold, silver, or copper in your belts, no bag for the journey, or an extra tunic, or sandals or staff, for the worker deserves his provisions. Whenever you enter a town or village, find out who is worthy there and stay with them until you leave. As you enter the house, give it greetings. And if the house is worthy, let your peace come on it, but if it is not worthy, let your peace return to you.

> And if anyone will not welcome you or listen to your message, shake the dust off your feet as you leave that house or that town.
> - Matthew 10:1, 5-14

Let's recap:

1. Jesus gives them *authority* to do what he did:

2. *Preach* and *proclaim* the gospel - ("the Kingdom of heaven [God] is near").

3. Through their *presence* of the Father's Spirit (v. 20), set free the captives, oppressed, unclean, demon possessed.

4. Do this in such a way that nothing else distracts you from the purity of the mission and vision of the kingdom for others.

You would think that Jesus would stop here with his disciples. Everyone knows that the farther you outstretch your vision the weaker and more dissipated it becomes. Most also know that you don't just give anyone the keys to the house. Only those who have proven their integrity, intelligence, etc. But, Jesus seems to pick twelve incredibly unqualified men (most were the age of teenage boys), who had little track record other then being willing to leave everything for Him (which would actually seem like a negative today). He also doesn't stop with just the twelve.

—

Jesus' Extends His Mission to 72 Others

We see this done again in Luke 10, where Jesus sends out 72 with very similar instructions.

> Whenever you enter a town and the people welcome

> you, eat what is set before you. Heal the sick in that town and say to them, 'The kingdom of God has come upon you!'
> - Luke 10:8-9

They are also to *proclaim* the good news and have a healing *presence* to set people free.

After Jesus sends off his disciples and the 72 to go and live out his mission, John the Baptist starts to doubt if this is really Jesus the Messiah that they've been waiting for.

> Now when John heard in prison about the deeds Christ had done, he sent his disciples to ask a question: "Are you the one who is to come, or should we look for another?" Jesus answered them, "Go tell John what you *hear and see*. The blind see, the lame walk, lepers are cleansed, the deaf hear, the dead are raised, and the poor have good news *proclaimed* to them.
> - Matthew 11:2-6

Jesus responds by saying: The good news is being proclaimed to the poor, and through our presence the captives and oppressed are being set free. This is the mission of Jesus seen through his ministry, and the very same mission we are tasked with.

An Advantage After the Resurrection
Once Jesus is crucified and resurrected, we see him giving his mission away to his disciples (and us).
Jesus says in John 16 that he must go, but he is giving them an advantage by the coming of the Holy Spirit, who is our advocate.

> But I tell you the truth, it is to your *advantage* that I am going away. For if I do not go away, the *Advocate* will not come to you, but if I go, I will send him to you.

> And when he comes, he will prove the world wrong concerning sin and righteousness and judgment—concerning sin, because they do not believe in me; concerning righteousness, because I am going to the Father and you will see me no longer.
> - John 16:7-10

After this teaching on the Spirit, there are four different endings to after Jesus' resurrection.
The most well-known one falls in the account by Matthew. He says:

> Then Jesus came up and said to them, "All authority in heaven and on earth has been given to me. Therefore go and make disciples of all nations, baptizing them in the name of the Father and the Son and the Holy Spirit, teaching them to obey everything I have commanded you. And remember, I am with you always, to the end of the age."
> - Matthew 28:18-20

These are Jesus' final words to his twelve and other disciples. Jesus had shown at this point that there were other disciples, and that the gospel will be preached to the entire nation.
Therefore, this is his great commission to them, and also us today. It is broken into two components:

1. *Go* and *make* disciples (baptizing here was the proof of Jesus-followers).

This means to leave where they are and set up to be his witnesses. Therefore, we are still all called to follow the way, teachings, and life of Jesus while we are leaving to go spread the good news to all. However, we cannot forget the second part. Dallas Willard coined this the "great *omission*," instead of the great *commission* because of our disregard for the second part.

2. *Teach* them to obey.

This means that we don't just strive for conversions, or hand raises, but that if we are going to usher in the kingdom of God for people, we must also teach others what it means to follow Jesus. Teach people. Train them in the way of Jesus. We must play the long game in discipleship. This is why the local church is so important. We have the opportunity to teach and equip people to be followers of Jesus for the long haul.

—

Mission = Proclamation and Presence of Love
The mission of Jesus is love. This is a fulfillment of the mission of God for humanity, which is his ultimate love for His creation. This mission is extended to us by: prioritizing a Jesus-love through proclamation and presence so that people are able to engage with the Kingdom of God.

The two areas that displayed Jesus' mission were completely submerged in love. Jesus exuded love in his proclamation (sometimes harsh love, sometimes gracious love), and also in his presence. God is love. Jesus is God, Jesus is love. His life, ministry, and sacrifice is the definition of love. That is why Jesus says:

> "…the mark of love is those who lay down their own lives for others."
> - John 13:34-35

—

What's Our Role Now?

> Who is Apollos, really? Or who is Paul? Servants through whom you came to believe, and each of us in

the ministry the Lord gave us. I planted, Apollos watered, but God caused it to grow. So neither the one who plants counts for anything, nor the one who waters, but God who causes the growth. The one who plants and the one who waters work as one, but each will receive his reward according to his work. We are *coworkers* belonging to God. You are God's field, God's building. According to the grace of God given to me, like a skilled master-builder I laid a foundation, but someone else builds on it. And each one must be careful how he builds. For no one can lay any *foundation* other than what is being laid, which is Jesus Christ.
- 1 Corinthians 3:5-11

We are to engage and be co-workers in Jesus' mission. To lay a foundation of Jesus Christ and his love. We are identified as followers of Jesus, as champions of his mission by our love. If we proclaim and have a presence of Jesus, they must be able to be identified by love. Otherwise, we are Pharisees or liars. Paul solidifies this by saying:

For the love of Christ *controls* us, since we have concluded this, that Christ died for all; therefore all have died. And he died for all so that those who live should no longer live for themselves but for him who died for them and was raised.
- 2 Corinthians 5:14-15

One commentator put it simply:

"Those verses are not referring to *our love* for Christ, though that may perhaps also be a motivation for mission, but rather to *Christ's love working through those* who are his people. He loves through us, and his love should cause us to reach out and identify with those who need the gospel."[16]
- James Boice

Do People Take Safety in Your Branches?
I'll wrap-up this idea of mission and love with a parable Jesus said of the mustard seed:

> "The kingdom of heaven is like a mustard seed that a man took and sowed in his field. It is the smallest of all the seeds, but when it has grown it is the greatest garden plant and becomes a tree, so that the *wild birds come and nest in its branches.*"
> - Matthew 13:31-32

Are we living our lives in such a way that there are wild birds taking nest, safety, and love in our branches?

James Boice told two contrasting stories that help us answer this question:
Here are two stories by which we can evaluate the presence or absence of the love of Christ for others in our lives.

"During the years I spent in Basel, Switzerland doing graduate study, I met a woman named Sheila. She had come from a bad background in England and had gone to Switzerland when still young in order to make a better life for herself. She was lonely. Having no one to turn to, she fell in with a young man who did not marry her but left her with a child. By the time I met her, the child was about four years old, and Sheila herself was on guard against most people and was very hostile to the church and Christianity.

In time, through the witness of the English-speaking community, she became a Christian, and about the time I left Switzerland to return to America she immigrated to Canada. My wife and I corresponded with her for about six months after she arrived in Canada and had the impression that she was not fitting in with any Christian group in her area. We went to visit her and found that we were right. We began to talk about her with various

Christian people we knew in her city. There was interest to a degree, but no real love. They told us, 'Oh, there is a very good church in our city.' They gave us the name. Sometimes it was a Presbyterian church, sometimes Baptist, sometimes independent. But in all our conversations no one said, 'Give me her name and address. I'll stop by and invite her to go with me on Sunday morning.'

Finally, being very unhappy, she left that city for another and (I am afraid) once again fell in with bad company. Eventually, in spite of much effort, we lost touch with her.

The second story is more promising. It was told at the Berlin Congress on Evangelism (1966) by the Rev. Fernando Vangioni. He said that he was in South America for a series of meetings, and after one of them a woman came to him and said, 'I wonder if you would take time to speak to a girl I am bringing to the meeting tomorrow night. She went to New York some years ago, full of hope, thinking that America was the land of opportunity. Instead of doing well she went through terrible times in the city. She was used by one man after another. All treated her badly. Now she has returned to this country very bitter and hostile to all forms of Christianity.' The evangelist said he would speak to her.

On the next night the girl was there. Vangioni said he had never looked into such hard eyes or listened to a voice so hostile. At last, seeing he was making no progress in talking with her, he asked, 'Do you mind if I pray for you?'

'Pray if you like,' the girl said, 'but don't preach to me. And don't expect me to listen.'

He began to pray, and as he prayed *he was greatly moved*. Something in the tragedy of her life caused tears to run down his face. At last he stopped. There was nothing to add. He said, 'All right, you can go now.'

But the girl did not go. Touched by that manifestation of love for her, she replied, 'No, I won't go. You can preach to me now. No man has ever cried for me before.'

We need to ask if we have ever been touched at all for one who is lost and ignorant of Christ's love. Do we say, 'We have a wonderful church; she (or he) should go there?' Or do we go out of our way to know and communicate? May our lives be indicative of Jesus' love, and the availability and beauty found in his Kingdom.

Reflection Question
Am I orchestrating who I was created to be, my career, spheres of influences, time and more to further the mission of Jesus on Earth?

Recommended Reading
- *Imitating Jesus* by Lewie Clark
- *The Tangible Kingdom* by Hugh Halter
- *The Gospel Comes with a Housekey* by Rosaria Butterfield
- *Surprise the World: Five Habits of Highly Missional People* by Michael Frost

community

If you obey my commandments, you will remain in my love, just as I have obeyed my Father's commandments and remain in his love…My commandment is this—to love one another just as I have loved you. No one has greater love than this—that one lays down his life for his friends…This I command you—to love one another

- John 15:10, 12-13, 17

> We have come to know love by this: that Jesus laid down his life for us; thus we ought to lay down our lives for our fellow Christians. But whoever has the world's possessions and sees his fellow Christian in need and shuts off his compassion against him, how can the love of God reside in such a person?
>
> - 1 John 3:16-17

Kintsugi is a beautiful Japanese art form. It takes broken pieces of ceramic or other materials, and uses golden, silver, lacquer/dust to reform the pieces into a complete bowl, plate, or other vessel.

As a philosophy, it treats "breakage and repair as part of the history of an object, rather than something to disguise." It is the very foundation for beauty to flourish.

How beautiful is that? Our brokenness is something that when repaired, is not something to disguise or hide, but to show as a part of our story and history.

Just like Kintsugi, there is beauty in broken things being put together as a whole in a holistic way to create or display something much bigger than just one piece.

Similarly, a mosaic is beautiful, but what makes it beautiful is the meticulous time it takes for the artist to put together several colored pieces and shapes and sizes all together to form one beautiful piece of art.

I don't have to create a compelling argument for you all to know that each one of us is deeply flawed—and there are things in our life that we see, experience or partake in that we know are wrong. Malevolence, suffering, and pain are in the world. We do things each day that we know are bad, or sinful. Sometimes you may even wrestle with the frustration that we can just wake up the next day, knowing exactly what we ought to do, and still not even come close.

Here is the most encouraging news: God knows this, and he's done something incredible about it.

Since the beginning of creation, in Genesis 2:18 it says "it is not good for man to be alone." We as humans, created in the image of God, a God who is triune, meaning he is in community as well, calls us to be in community. We are social creatures. No person is a complete island. Sure some are more introverted, but there is power in togetherness.

—

Infants Need to be Held
Several years back the Times magazine (science section) did a piece on the staggering infant mortality rate in orphanages, in some cases 30-40%.

In an effort to determine why there were such high rates, the overwhelming consensus was that babies (0-5) did not receive enough human stimulation in group residential care to develop to their full capacity.

They argued that:

> nurturing is necessary for the brain to learn to connect human contact with pleasure. This association is one of the foundations of empathy: We connect first through soothing touch and shared smiles. Sadly, babies raised in orphanages often begin to fear touch and avoid it. Without having intensive, repeated, *loving contact* with the same one or two people, they simply can't make the proper connections. They don't get enough repetition with particular people to build in bonding. And that can spell trouble later in life as this early touch helps provide the template for all relationships thereafter.

Whether Christian, Agnostic, Atheist, etc., you cannot deny the social construct within a human's wiring that we require others for survival. Babies are a prime example of their full dependence on others for their survival.

To plunge even deeper, humans aren't just social, but

also extremely malleable people. We become who we are around, idolize, spend time with, etc. We are always becoming something, just as we are always worshiping something. We are far more tribal than most would think. You may even have started to feel this as you navigate the political strife that has invaded America over the last few decades.

With all this in mind, community and togetherness is integral in following Jesus.

Community is more than an Avocado Add-On
People like to think of community as an add-on, like avocado on a burger.

But to be honest, community is much more like the water in concrete mix. It is fascinating how you can have a bag of weak powdery cement mix, then all you have to do is add water and it creates a reactions which gives the whole thing structure and strength—thus solid concrete. This is how integral community is in following Jesus. It is not an add-on, but instead it is one of the *primary, cohesive ingredients* at the very core and DNA of Jesus followers.

Community is a *must* for those who follow Jesus.

Community is our declaration of the church's involvement in our pursuit of Jesus. The church, or community of Jesus-followers was created to help followers of Jesus do this together. The church exists to help followers of Jesus pursue relationship, spiritual formation, and mission, together. Jesus didn't just call the disciples to head out on their own, and do it alone. He created "His church" to do all of these things together. We call this community, body of Christ, or fellow believers, saints, etc.

If you were to read the gospels, you would realize that you are to be with Jesus, become like Him, and even live out His mission. But, right after this Jesus sent the Holy Spirit and created his "Church." We as humans, created in the image of God, represent a DNA that is from the fabric of a God who is a communal God.

—

What Does This Comm*unity* Look Like?
A lot of us may struggle with this question because many of us have had different experiences with the Church already! To top that off, the best starting point in Jesus' words is prioritizing *unity*. How can we prioritize unity if everyone has different ideas/experiences with community? We may not realize this, but a lot of what we deem "good community" is just our own history or dream of what we think true community should look like. Dietrich Bonhoeffer was spot-on when he said:

> "The person who loves *their dream* of community will destroy community, but the person who loves *those around them* will create community."
> - Dietrich Bonhoeffer, *Life Together*

So the best starting point for understanding and engaging community is:

1. To *understand* Jesus heart for unity, and

2. to *acknowledge* where our own dreams, past experiences, and assumptions about community (and the Church) lie.

Once we see the depth and importance of those in our lives, we can come to the table with healthy intentions.

Community in terms of the Church was the crescendo of God's plan after Jesus does his job on earth. We can't forget that Jesus intentionally left earth and ascended to heaven after his death, burial, and resurrection. He was not *abandoning* God's great narrative. Instead, he was *making a way* for his Church to fill the earth and live out his great commission.

Jesus shows us his desire for this in John 17, as he prays one of his longest prayers hours before his death,

> "I am not praying only on their [disciples] behalf, but also on behalf of those who believe in me through their testimony, that they will all be one, just as you, Father, are in me and I am in you. I pray that they will be in us, so that the world will believe that you sent me. The glory you gave to me I have given to them, that they may be one just as we are one—I in them and you in me—that they may be completely one, *so that* the world will know that you sent me, and you have loved them just as you have loved me."
> - John 17:20-23

Jesus' prayer towards the end of his ministry is yearning for God the Father to create a unified church of believers. *So that* they would be a sign/wonder to the world based on their unity which is a symbol of the Trinity's unity. Jesus prays one prayer at the end of his ministry on earth for future believers, and his priority is *unity*. This is so timely for where we are right now in our world.

Politics, Misinformation, and Chaos

It is an unprecedented time for not just information, but misinformation, and disinformation. You don't have to be a genius to go online and realize that everyone has an agenda, bias or stance, and that it is affecting the information we receive. We are in a world of information, but *information* does not always lead to *formation*.

For example, just because a teenager has access to the entire interweb does not make them better off, or even wiser. Yes, you can google that ambiguous movie star's height in 2 seconds, but Google isn't just going to make you a better person, or a more loving person, or a more unity-driven person.

Even worse, misinformation and disinformation are able to rally an even greater deal of harm to our culture. Though this may seem discouraging, it is actually a ripe time for followers of Jesus to be more attractive than they would normally be. There is nothing more attractive today in the midst of our cancel culture and noisy world, than a group of people who are *unified* in a way in which people are able to see the love of God.

The unification of our community, and the love with which we love each other is a *sign* and *wonder* for the world we currently live in. Jesus has been clear about this:

> "I give you a new commandment—to love one another. Just as I have loved you, you also are to love one another. Everyone will know *by this* that you are my disciples—if you have love for one another."
> - John 13:34-35

People want to see miracles, and you know what is a miracle? One democrat voter and one republican voter loving each other radically, sitting in the same church together, serving alongside one another, inviting one another into their home for dinner, listening intently to one another, fighting their own biases to understand where each person's heart is. We do all of the above in our mission together because it not only helps us, it helps others around us. It is the testimony of God's power through our love and pursuit of unity.

—

Togetherness is God's Plan

He doesn't have a Plan B. Jesus went up to heaven, gave us his Holy Spirit, and this is his plan, that Christ would be the head, and we would submit as his body, and as his body, people would be able to see and know him by our unity and our love. This is important because our unity and our love is a sign and testifying analogy of God's love and unity in himself, the trinity. It is a sign to the world, testifying not only to our relationships with each other, but also with God.

Even "the world" can see signs, by love and unity, and these are the heart and soul of the disciples' mission to the world—consequently the world's only hope. Everyone will know we are followers of Jesus if you have love for one another. It is shocking that a way of noticing the church is by their love for one another.

Are We A Community Worth Being A Part of?

It is common for a community of Jesus followers to want people to find Jesus and get plugged into his church, but would that person actually *be loved* in our church?

We have to ask ourselves, if we are going out and reaching people to be a part of our community, are we a community worth being a part of? Are we testifying to the unity and love of Jesus and his Father? Do we live with Holy Spirit power in such a way that it's noticeable? Or do we do things just like the "world" as Paul says: slandering, gossip, malice, sexual immortality, deception, lying, selfishness, etc (Colossians 3:5).

Jesus' Prays for His Desires

> "Father, I *want* those you have given me to be with me where I am, so that they can see my glory that you gave me because you loved me before the creation of the world. Righteous Father, even if the world does not know you, I know you, and these men know that you sent me. I made known your name to them, and I will continue to make it known, so that the love you

have loved me with may be in them, and I may be in them."
- John 17:24-26

Jesus' final words in this prayer are different from his first. He doesn't just pray for the Father's will to be done, but says that he "wants." This shows Jesus' desire in this prayer for us, and it is: that his disciples will experience the love of God the Father, through Jesus' love for them, that will then be displayed to the entire world.

Jesus knows that the Father's love will change the world if this love can be laid upon the disciples in their relationships. This love is what helps us achieve this unity that Jesus is aiming for. But this love is dependent on their *own unity* with Jesus, and Jesus' unity with God the Father. In the same way, God gave us the church to accomplish his work as co-labors of the Holy Spirit. We are never to stray from the love of God to accomplish our own dreams or desires.

Community (in Jesus' mind), has the simplest foundation. Its rooted in unity and love, and we will see this similar mindset as we look into the rest of the New Testament at the idea of "Church."

The Ekklesia

The future disciples, or the Church, is known most commonly in the Bible as *Ekklesia* in Greek, and is used 114 times exclusively in the NT NET Bible. However, in this fashion it is usually referring more to the *gathering of people* than a social entity or organization. So the "Church," a community of Jesus followers is to be a *gathering of people* marked by unity and love.

The church is to be identified more by their love and unity, than their social media or their budget or their building, or even their programs.

Jesus communicates that through our unity and love for

one another, we emulate and reveal the unity and love of the triune God, or the trinity. This, in tandem with the Holy Spirit's power is a true fulfillment of the type of community Jesus had in mind. A.W. Tozer gives a great example of this *gathering of people* being like a house, and the Spirit of God being electricity:

> "Unity is necessary for the outpouring of the Spirit of God. If you have 120 volts of electricity coming into your house but you have broken wiring, you may turn on the switch, but nothing works – no lights come on, the stove doesn't warm, the radio doesn't turn on. Why? Because you have broken wiring. The power is ready to do its work…, but where there is broken wiring, there is no power. Unity is necessary among the children of God if we are going to know the flow of power…to see God do His wonders."[17]

—

A Different Looking Church

We know that unity has been the problem since Jesus' time. The disciples had arguments over who was better and would be closer to Jesus; they were no different. There is a constant battle against unity and love.

Therefore, we have to remember that our unity and love as community of Jesus followers is still called to submit to Jesus. We must approach the idea of being a part of the "body of Christ" with humility, and that in our service and submission, we fulfill Jesus' desire to become the "least among us".

> "God [the Father] has put *all things* under the authority of Christ and has made him head over all things for the *benefit* of the church. And the church is his body; it is made full and complete by Christ, who fills all things everywhere with himself."
> - Ephesians 1:22-23 (and Colossians 1)

Later, Ephesians 5 says that Jesus is the *savior* of the church, and that the church *submits* to Him. This idea of Jesus' authority and our (the churches) submission has a beautiful foundation of a marriage-covenant. Jesus made a promise to to save us and never leave us. We are to submit to our groom (Jesus) and be his bride (the Church). If we take this marriage-covenant symbol seriously, we realize just how incredibly intimate this relationship is.

—

The Church is Jesus' Wife

Most of us have heard (or personally said) the line:

> "I love Jesus, but I don't like church," or "I don't need it," or "They aren't like Jesus."

But let me ask you, how would you respond if someone told you:

> "I really love you, but I can't stand your spouse, I want nothing to do with them. Can just the two of us hang out? And never with your spouse?"

What would you say? What would you feel? I think any of us would be pretty frustrated at someone saying that to us. Personally, I think it should make us question if they even like us, because they are the closest thing to us.

In the same way, we don't get to say "I love Jesus," and hate his bride. We don't get to spend time with Jesus and never with His church. We can't love the head of the Church and hate the body. Loving the church of broken people as Jesus did is a *non-negotiable* for those who claim Jesus as Lord. They are together as one. This is the same reason as we can't hate God the Father and just love Jesus. We can't love Jesus and hate the Holy Spirit. They are one, and in our love, we are to strive to love them together, three-in-one.

A lot of us know that the church is full of broken people, who do broken things. But just remember, the head of that body is Jesus, and he doesn't want you slandering his wife.

Our call, when we follow Jesus, is to be a part of the body of Christ, and follow Him, *together*. In this we grow closer to him, and become more like Him naturally. The Church's goal of unity and love is also the fruit of pursuing it together.

Jesus rarely did anything alone, and when he sent people out, he sent them in twos. Paul's letters always reach out to fellow workers for Christ. Our faith is not just our own, but it is shown, expressed, and grown in community.

The Western world has done a terrible disservice to revealing the *communal* aspect of faith because we are such an *individualistic* society. But, the church is to be a social and a together-type group of people. We are to be marked by love and unity in such a way that it is a sign and wonder to the world.

—

The Early Church
The start of the Church has a powerful start. The Holy Spirit (like Jesus promised) came upon the Apostles, and they preached the gospel of repentance, 3000 people come to faith, and the community of "believers" is established. The next two verses after this start say:

> All the believers devoted themselves to the apostles' teaching, and to fellowship, and to sharing in meals (including the Lord's Supper), and to prayer. A deep sense of awe came over them all.
> - Acts 2:42-43

The early church was a radical showcase of unified love and awe to the world around them. People were able to see a divine, tangible love from the love and unity that the followers of Jesus showed to one another.

The foundation of our relationship with Jesus, our spiritual formation, and mission is all rooted in the unifying love his Church is to embody as they live out his way *together*.

Together, we are able to be with Jesus, and encourage one another to: be in prayer, heal in areas that we aren't being honest with God about, be held accountable as we lament sin, and encourage the love of Jesus. Together, we are able to become more like Jesus, by seeing people around us become more like him and growing a passion for more of Jesus. Together, we are able to live out Jesus' mission through a kingdom movement of proclamation and presence in our little areas, workplaces, bars, and gyms.

We do all of these things better, together, and Jesus gives us his "Body" because he is using it for the future of the world, not just haphazardly. Jesus' first allusion about the Church to Peter says:

> I tell you that you are Peter, and on this rock I will build my church, and the *gates of Hades will not overpower it*. I will give you the keys of the kingdom of heaven.
> - Matthew 16:18-19

Our togetherness through unity and love is one of the greatest apologetics for ourselves and others in the world today. N.T. Wright, a prominent scholar on the Bible and first century Judaism says:

> The Christian faith spread in the early centuries, despite the Romans trying to stamp it out, because of *"ordinary"* people living in an *extraordinary* way: caring for people — especially the poor — even when they were not related to them; giving people medical treatment, education and so on (which had been reserved for the rich or the elite before). People were

astonished. They didn't know it was *possible* to live like that!

Another particular point was the early church's insistence on sexual holiness. Again, people had no idea it was *possible* or *desirable* to live like that.

The other thing that made a big impact was the church's strong belief in the coming resurrection (which…went closely with their belief that what you do with your present body matters a lot).

Wouldn't it be good if the church today was known in the same way?

'Many assume that Christianity is about a big bully in the sky who basically hates us but (fortunately for us) decided to take out his bad temper on someone else … The Bible doesn't say "God so hated the world" but "*God so loved the world.*"'[18]

Reverential Awe
As shown earlier, the early church, was marked by a few distinct practices and characteristics. But the most fascinating piece of this time is the result:

> *Reverential awe* came over everyone, and many wonders and miraculous signs came about by the apostles. All who believed were together and held everything in common,
> - Acts 2:43

The reverential awe is a decrystallization of the norm. It is seeing the extraordinary things done by the Spirit in the hearts of ordinary people. This is our baseline as a community. If we are truly walking in the way of Jesus and his idea for the church, we will surely receive a reverential awe for what God is doing through normal people.

May we be encouraged to be the true, radical church that Jesus desires out of us through the leading of the Holy Spirit.

Reflection Questions
Are we seeking to pursue the means required to be in reverential awe of Jesus, his love, and mercy towards our community?

Are we in awe of how he is working and will work through us for his kingdom advancement?

Recommended Reading:
- *Life Together* by Dietrich Bonhoeffer
- *Radical Together* by David Platt
- *Letters to the Church* by Francis Chan

tetelestai

"Then when he received the sour wine Jesus said,
'It is finished,'
and he bowed his head and gave up his spirit."

- John 19:30

"It is finished."

This word, *tetelestai* occurs only two times in the Bible—John 19:28 and 19:30.

The word *tetelestai* was also written on business documents or receipts in New Testament times to show indicating that a bill had been paid in full.

Let us **never** forget that Jesus has paid our debts.

He has paid for our sins in full. Now let us go live out this freedom by loving others as he does for us.

appendix a | VIM

The process of Spiritual formation is from Dallas Willard's *Renovation of the Heart*, which is a three-step acronym: VIM.

Vision
The first step of pursuing spiritual formation is to yearn for a lens where we:

> See Jesus' gospel of the kingdom offered to me in my struggles and the need of others.

Questions to Ask:
- Do I have a vision of the kingdom that is true and life altering?
- What area do I need to become more like the image of Jesus, and why?
- What does Jesus' kingdom have that I want to be a part of, engaged with, and passionate about?

Our foundation for spiritual formation is rooted in who we are and our thoughts, feelings, dispositions, choices (the inner life). It is not just how we act, which is a common mistake in the Christian culture. Focusing on how we act is legalism and hypocrisy, like the Pharisees, if we let the gospel skip our heart and mind.

Our vision should be *life, now and forever, in the range of God's will*—partaking in God's plan and relationships with him (one in Christ) through being born again, and participating by our actions in what God is doing now in our lifetime on earth.

This vision is yearned for in our relationships with the Holy Spirit, giving us relationship with Jesus and clarity of his kingdom.

The vision for the kingdom and the gospel is our priority.

Intention
The vision of life in the kingdom through reliance upon Jesus makes it possible for us to intend to live in the kingdom as he did. We intend to live in and foster the kingdom of God by intending to obey his precise example and teachings of Jesus. No one can actually believe the truth about Jesus and his gospel without trusting him by intending to obey him.

You can no more trust Jesus and not intend to obey him than you could trust your doctor, or mechanic and not intend to follow their advice. If you don't intend to follow their advice, you don't trust them.

Our intention is choosing with my heart to rely on God to help me become the kind of person he's shown me that I can be in a specific area of my life.

Questions to Ask:
- What am I fighting against?
- What do I not want to give up?
- How do I engage my heart to God and relinquish control?

When Jesus says "Those who want to find life will lose it" means that those who think they are in control of their life will ultimately realize how little control they actually have, and therefore are drawn to their knees, and to surrender.

Our intentions are heart choices and decisions to renovate our current area of our life to match that of Jesus'.

Means.
The means is:

Applying specific spiritual disciplines and habits as God's means of grace in my focused area of growth.

These become the components of the Rule of Life. This is

where our spiritual disciplines and habits come into play. We have to learn what disciplines can be formative for our faith (bible reading, prayer, fasting, silence, sabbath, etc.) and incorporate that into a rhythm (or rule) of life.

Questions to Ask:
- What habits can I engage with that help me develop habits of love, and transformation for myself and those around?
- What areas of my life need more habits/disciplines?
- What areas should I seek to find more meaningful expressions of Jesus?
- What are those habits and disciplines I am going to put into place?

appendix b | rule of life

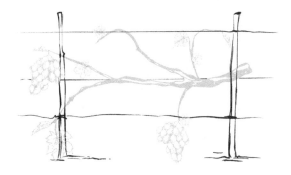

A Rule of Life is essentially a set of principles and practices that compliment the commitment you have made with Jesus. This idea originated from a group of monastic, Egyptian communities known as the Desert Fathers in the third century AD. This community believed the Rule of Life was established to shift and grow their faith into habits and rhythms each day, month, year, etc. The idea of a rule of life is best understood by a trellis. A trellis provides structure and health for the vine to grow and have underpinnings so that it may climb to much higher heights without toppling over or snapping..

Every follower of Jesus needs a trellis as they learn to abide in the vine (Jesus). It is crucial to craft a personal/family rule of life. In this, we cultivate an intentional spiritual growth plan that is able to be focused on and observed.

This idea is from Jesus' reiteration of the OT *Shema*. Again, The *Shema* was a foundational passage for the Israelites found in Deuteronomy 6:4-9 (NET):

> Hear, O Israel: The Lord is our God, the Lord is one! You must love the Lord your God with your whole mind, your whole being [heart and soul], and all your strength [body]. These words I am commanding you today must be kept in mind, and you must teach them to your children and speak of them as you sit in your house, as you walk along the road, as you lie down, and as you get up. You should tie them as a reminder on your forearm and fasten them as symbols on your forehead. Inscribe them on the doorframes of your houses and gates.

Jesus references this in three Gospels (Matt 22:37-39; Mark 12:29-31; Luke 10:27).

Below is Mark 12:29-31:

> Which commandment is the most important of all?" Jesus answered, "The most important is: 'Listen, Israel, the Lord our God, the Lord is one. Love the Lord your God with all your heart, with all your soul, with all your mind, and with all your strength.' The second is: 'Love your neighbor as yourself.'

Therefore, our Rule of Life has several components that accomplish a holistic rule of life that seeks to grow our heart, soul, mind and strength towards loving God and our neighbor more.

—

spiritual

Relationship
What are my normal rhythms and habits cultivating a deeper intimacy and relationship with Jesus? How is my heart/soul continually growing and connecting with God? How am I creating opportunities to enjoy God?

Examples/Tips:
- Prayer (Daily, listening 15 mins a day for God's voice)
- Worship (Worship music, Nature, etc.)
- Solitude with Jesus (escaping all distractions daily, and/or an hour a week in silence)
- Sabbath (Centered around a quality chunk of time devoted to your relationship with Jesus).

Spiritual Formation
What are my normal rhythms and habits cultivating my formation to becoming more like Jesus in my posture, and thoughts?

Examples/Tips:
- Prayer (Yearning for the Spirit to change/renovate areas of our hearts)
- Reading/Bible reading (Reading books, and God's word with a focus on being transformed by it)
- Solitude (Because it allows your to practice more of the lifestyle/rhythm of Jesus)
- Sabbath (It allows you to rest as Jesus rested)
- Coach/Mentor (Someone who keeps you accountable and can push you deeper and more intensively into the emulation of Jesus)
- Mental/Emotional health (*See section under Physical below)

Missional
What are my normal rhythms and habits that keep me mobilized and empowered in my actions to live out the mission of Jesus around me?

Examples/Tips:
- An Intentional Third-Space (A space where you go consistently each week and be among not-yet Christians/Sojourners.

- Generosity Budget (Make room in your budget to be generous to people)
- Hospitality (Find ways to show hospitality to all people, dinner, backyard party, etc.)
- Missional Focused Community (A community that takes mission seriously)

---

vocational

Work Schedule
Do I have integrity in my weekly hours, projects, and schedule? Have I set up clear boundaries for my work schedule? Do I have my schedule set in a way that best honors my daily rhythms and capacity? Do I take my Sabbath seriously?

Examples/Tips:
- Establish a weekly schedule/rhythm to be efficient with your unique work style (if applicable)
- Calendar your Sabbath, turn your phone off, never plan anything that would be taxing, or involve a "work mindset" on the Sabbath.
- Schedule time/set a week amount to pray, and read.

Work/Life Balance
Have I communicated and established an agreeable work-life balance with my family, boss, and others?

Examples/Tips:
- Communicate clear expectations with those who are frequently in your life rhythms-- roommates, spouse, children, family, close friends.
- Set-up clear boundaries that are realistic from both ends of work and life.

Vacation/Rest
Do I have my vacation schedule out in an adequate amount of time? Do I plan my vacations in such a way that I come back rested and refreshed? Do I plan for specific times of rest within the calendar year, holidays, specific seasons of life?

Examples:
- Plan the large vacation dates, a minimum 3-4 months out.
- Cultivate a period of rest within the vacation and/or the tail end of the trip.
- Find opportunities to vacation that are lightweight and can be consistent.

—

physical

Health
Am I seeing a doctor, dentist regularly? Do I have any areas, issues, or problems that I am neglecting?

Exercise
Am I active and exercising in a way that allows my body to feel good, and be able to accomplish the work and goals God has entrusted me with? Am I active in such a way that I believe I am being a good steward of my earthly body?

Diet (Food/Drink)
Am I consuming food and drink that is contributing to the healthy and stewardship of my body? Am I giving way to any continual patterns of unhealthy eating, excessive drinking, or damaging eating habits?

Sleep
Am I sleeping a regular and consistent amount? Am I

creating boundaries so that I may have adequate amounts of sleep?

Stress/Hurry
Am I setting up my days, and weeks to not be in a hurry? Do I allow physical, mental, and emotional downtime? Does my body have any signs that I am hurried or stressed?

Mental/Emotional Health
Am I mentally/emotionally healthy? Is there anything I am fearful of? Resenting? Avoiding? Unhealed from? Do I feel free and restored from any of my past, family of origin situations, abuse/trauma? If not, how am I cultivating a path of healing, redemption, and/or reconciliation?

—

relational/others

How are the relationships around me? Am I living in agreeance to the priorities I've set? How am I actively loving my neighbor around me? How am I seeking to live in community where I can love others and be loved?

Counseling
Do I have a consistent meeting with a licensed/trusted counselor who is able to help we work through things that may not be addressed in the church setting?

Marriage
Am I taking continual steps to love my spouse in a selfless manner, reflecting Jesus' love for the church? Am I taking weekly date-nights/intentional marriage time? Am I being intentional around ways to love my spouse in their love language/style? Am I receiving legitimate coaching from others whose marriages I respect and look up to? Am I

honoring my spouse in intimacy and sex?

Kids
Do I cultivate opportunities to minister and love my kids well? Do I spend enough time with them each week? Are there unique ways I am helping them adapt a rule or life, or family rhythms that are helping the family love Jesus together?

Immediate Family
Do I maintain a healthy and consistent relationship with my immediate family? Have I established healthy boundaries for my family and their lives with my own?

---

financial/stewardship

How am I stewarding the money, gifts, and blessings God has given me, and being generous to others?

Debt
Do I have, or are considering taking out loans, especially unnecessary loans due to cultural pressure? Am I taking out more debt before paying off my initial debts? Do I have a serious, and aggressive plan to pay-off any debt I owe? Do I follow the plan?

Generosity
Do I have a budget for ways to be generous to my friends, community, neighbors, missionaries, and benevolent opportunities? Am I giving to the point where it hurts or makes me uncomfortable? Am I a joyful giver? Does my checking account reflect someone who is radically generous? Am I tithing/giving back to God a biblical share of what he calls me to? Are there people and organizations that I should be consistently supporting? Do I pray about the money I spend?

appendix c | recommended reading

Relationship
- *The Praying Life* by Paul E. Miller
- *The Power of Extraordinary Prayer* by Robert Bakke
- *Emotionally Healthy Spirituality* by Pete Scazzero
- *Sacred Pathways* by Gary Thomas
- *In the Name of Jesus* by Henri Nouwen

Formation
- *Renovation of the Heart* by Dallas Willard
- *The Cost of Discipleship* by Dietrich Bonhoeffer
- *Celebration of Discipline* by Richard Foster
- *Gentle & Lowly* by Dane Ortlund
- *The Ruthless Elimination of Hurry* by John Mark Comer
- *Invitation to a Journey: A Road Map for Spiritual Formation* by M. Robert Mulholland Jr.

Mission
- *Imitating Jesus* by Lewie Clark
- *The Tangible Kingdom* by Hugh Halter
- *The Gospel Comes with a Housekey* by Rosaria Butterfield
- *Surprise the World: Five Habits of Highly Missional People* by Michael Frost

Community
- *Life Together* by Dietrich Bonhoeffer
- *Radical Together* by David Platt
- *Letters to the Church* by Francis Chan

notes

[1] The Bible translation used is the NET, unless otherwise noted.

[2] A.W. Tozer, *The Knowledge of the Holy* (New York: HarperCollins, 1978), 1.

[3] Dallas Willard, Jan Johnson (2015). "Hearing God Through the Year: A 365-Day Devotional", p.307, InterVarsity Press

[4] Richard J. Foster, *Celebration of Discipline: The Path to Spiritual Growth*

[5] Peter Scazzero. https://www.emotionallyhealthy.org/how-healthy-is-your-experience-of-living-out-of-loving-union-with-jesus/

[6] Paul E. Miller. *A Praying Life: Connecting with God in a Distracting World*. 2017. Ch. 5

[7] ibid.

[8] Richard J. Foster. *The Celebration of Discipline The Path to Spiritual Growth*. p. 33

[9] Robert Bakke. *The Power of Extraordinary Prayer*. 2000.

[10] Henri J. M. Nouwen. *The Only Necessary Thing*, p. 39

[11] M. Robert Mulholland Jr.. *Invitation to a Journey: A Road Map for Spiritual Formation*. p. 42

[12] Dallas Willard. *Renovation of the Heart*. p. 66

[13] ibid.

[14] The Daredevil of Niagara Falls https://www.smithsonianmag.com/history/the-daredevil-of-niagara-falls-110492884/

[15] Paraphrase of John 1:29

[16] James Boice, *Foundations of the Christian Faith: A Comprehensive & Readable Theology Christ's Love.* p. 655

[17] A.W. Tozer. *Tozer on Christian Leadership,* 2001.

[18] N.T. Wright - https://christianchronicle.org/ordinary-people-living-in-an-extraordinary-way/

Made in the USA
Middletown, DE
10 November 2024